By Esther I. Wei & Alyssa F. Chen

WE'RE ALL DIFFERENT KINDS OF NUTS

Book **1** | Where Do You Get Your Energy?

Who are you calling a nut?

Nutmoji™
Nutmoji.com

This booklet is dedicated to our families, who drive us nuts and whom we love.

We're All Different Kinds of Nuts: Where Do You Get Your Energy?
by Esther I. Wei and Alyssa F. Chen

Published by Relational Repair
www.Nutmoji.com
Copyright © 2022 Esther I. Wei and Alyssa F. Chen

Cover and book design by Sterling Chen

ISBN: 979-8-9852865-0-2

Part 1
Nutty Energy

Each of us was created by God with a special mix of gifts and talents. God designed us to be relational and fruitful, to reflect his image and glory. Each of us does this in our own God-given way.

A big clue to understanding how God made each of us unique is to become aware of what *gives* us energy and what *drains* our energy.

Energy Givers are activities, people, or situations that replenish and energize us. They provide a positive boost, leaving us happy and refreshed. We would seek out—or welcome—these scenarios even if we didn't have to.

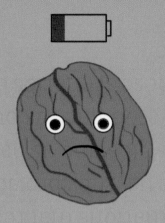

Energy Drainers are activities, people, or situations that leave us tired and grouchy. We try to avoid them. They are the things we participate in—or endure—only because we feel we must.

Nutmoji Energy Profile Activity

List your Energy Givers and your Energy Drainers. Together, the two lists form your Energy Profile. Try to identify at least 10 items each. Your Energy Profile provides clues as to how God made you unique.

CREATE YOUR ENERGY PROFILE

Energy Givers	Energy Drainers
1)	1)
2)	2)
3)	3)
4)	4)
5)	5)
6)	6)
7)	7)
8)	8)
9)	9)
10)	10)

Tip 1: Pay attention to our internal activation states.*

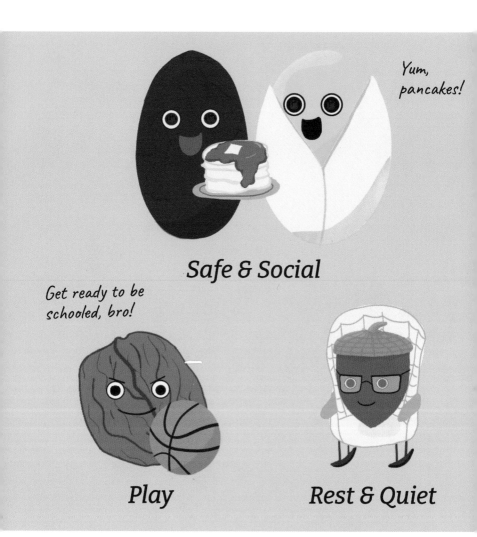

Safe & Social

Play

Rest & Quiet

These are signs of **Energy Givers**.

*Adapted from the following: Dana, D. (2018). *The polyvagal theory in therapy: Engaging the rhythm of regulation.* W.W. Norton & Company.

These are signs of **Energy Drainers**.

Porges, S.W. (2011). *The polyvagal theory: Neurophysiological foundations of emotions, attachment, communication, and self-regulation*. W.W. Norton & Company.

Tip 2: Listen to the messages our emotions are sending.

Safe & Social	Play	Rest & Quiet
Happy	Alert	Calm
Grateful	Adventurous	Peaceful
Affectionate	Eager	Relaxed
Compassionate	Curious	Understood
Accepted	Surprised	Quiet

What words match our emotional experience? Our feelings offer further hints about what is going on inside us.

Fight or Flight	Freeze	Collapse & Conserve
Angry	Scared	Sad
Frustrated	Stressed	Numb
Tense	Overwhelmed	Withdrawn
Irritated	Panicky	Tired
Disgusted	Anxious	Depressed

Our feelings naturally ebb and flow.

When we can sense our emotions, think clearly, function well, and respond flexibly, we are within our **Windows of Tolerance**.*

When we are overwhelmed by a situation, we may be stretched beyond our windows. That's when we tend to respond rigidly or chaotically.

Increasing our Energy Givers over time can help expand our windows, increasing our capacity to handle life.

*Window of Tolerance concept adapted from Siegel, D. (2020). *The developing mind: How relationships and the brain interact to shape who we are.* (3rd ed.) Guilford Press.

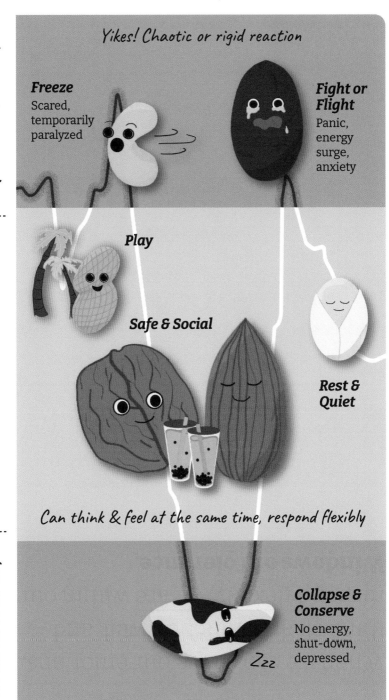

NUTTY ENERGY PROFILES

Name: *Walnut*

Energy Givers	Energy Drainers

Energy Givers

1) *Hiking*

2) *Library visits*

3) *Games, friends*

4) *Watching great athletes, performers*

5) *Guitar, singing*

Energy Drainers

1) *Waiting in line*

2) *Remaking decisions*

3) *Shopping*

4) *Doing things out of obligation*

Name: Peanut

Energy Givers

1) Appreciation

2) Chatting with friends

3) Reading

4) Staying at nice hotels

5) Checking off items on my to-do list

Energy Drainers

1) Redoing tasks

2) Working too much

3) Arguing

4) Hosting

Name: Pistachio

Energy Givers

1) Getting hugs

2) Cooking

3) Friend time

4) Stuffed animals

Energy Drainers

1) School

2) Large parties

3) Hiking

Some Energy Drainers in life are unavoidable. Mild to moderate stress is needed for motivation, learning, and productivity. However, overwhelming or chronic stress can damage our bodies, leading to all sorts of problems.

Our bodies and minds need regular breaks from work and stress. By paying attention to our Energy Profiles, we can choose the self-care options that will bring true refreshment and rest.

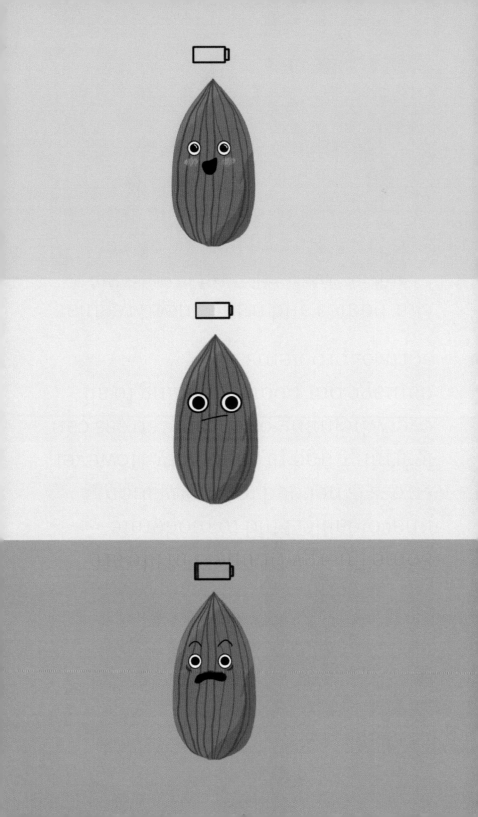

Increasing the regularity and frequency of Energy Givers and decreasing Energy Drainers will help us achieve a better rhythm in our lives, enhancing our capacity and overall contentment.

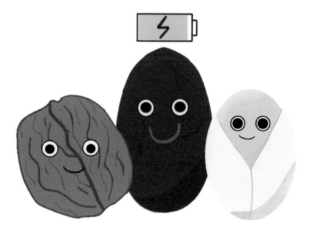

Part 2
Nut So Different

We all have different Energy Profiles because we are not the same kind of nuts.

And...because of our differences, we tend to drive each other a little nutty!

When frustrated with others, we may wonder why they are the way they are—why can't they be more like us?

We don't have to agree, act, or think exactly the same way. We each have varying views, feelings, desires, strengths, and vulnerabilities.

The challenge is to recognize our *own* nutty-ness and make room for other types of nuts.

Nutty character traits that shape our Energy Profiles are often relative. We are more or less of something depending on who we compare ourselves to.

Our "nutty-ness" lies on a continuum, which shows a range in steps or degrees. The other nuts in our lives may not be trying to irritate us. They may simply be on a *different* spot than us on that continuum.

Some nuts are cooperative while other nuts are more competitive.

MORE COOPERATIVE

MORE COMPETITIVE

Let's play a cooperative game so we can be on the same team!

《Groan 》

DECIDES QUICKLY

DECIDES SLOWLY

Some nuts are faster while others are slower.

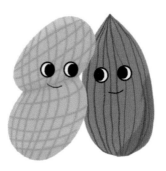

Thank you for pushing me to make plans earlier. It ended up being a great vacation!

MORE ORGANIZED

LESS ORGANIZED

LESS FLEXIBLE

MORE FLEXIBLE

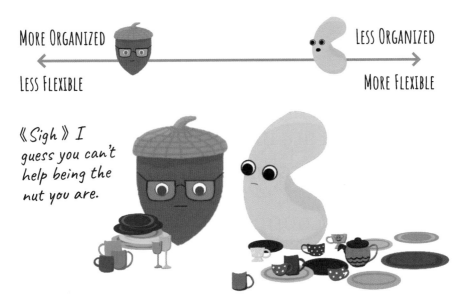

《Sigh》 I guess you can't help being the nut you are.

Some nuts are more organized while other nuts are more flexible.

HEY, EVERYONE!! I think I'm an INTROVERT too! I LOVE hanging out with all of you! When's our NEXT introvert group activity?

Um, you know introverts don't typically SEEK time in large groups, right?

You? An introvert?

《People get tired of other people? How can that be?》

VERY EXTROVERTED

MODERATELY EXTROVERTED

Extroverts tend to enjoy larger groups because they gain energy from being with people.

...and others are more introverted.

Peanut, you perk up a lot during social gatherings. I sure don't.

You might be an introvert —compared to Cashew. Perhaps you're a... "SHY" extrovert?

Solitude never bothered me anyway...

I must be a "SOCIAL" introvert. I like to help people (but then I need a nap).

MODERATELY INTROVERTED

VERY INTROVERTED

Introverts feel drained in those same settings. Introverts may need to spend some time alone or interact with fewer people to feel recharged.

We are each different by God's design. Kindly *accepting* the nuts around us for who they are can help everyone get along and move in a healthy direction.

You nuts go ahead and enjoy your time here together. I'll just go and be somewhere else by myself.

One last thing...
We're Nut Perfect

Focusing on areas that we *can* control—instead of what we can't— helps us to feel empowered instead of helpless.

Admitting our *own* nutty-ness can help ground us in humility when trying to cope with others' nutty behaviors.

Others may not be the way we want them to be, but they are their own kind of nutty.

The truth is: *None* of us are perfect, far from it.

We *all* have aspects that can drive others crazy at times. By remembering this truth, we can have more compassion for *other* people's quirks and mistakes. We can increase our capacity for kindness.

After all, in the end, we're all just different kinds of "nuts."

About the Authors

Esther I. Wei is a marriage and family therapist in northern California who enjoys helping others understand God's holistic development of their lives.

Alyssa F. Chen loves playing games and drinking bubble tea. She developed the Nutmoji characters and drew the book's illustrations during her sophomore and junior years of high school.

To learn more and to access downloadable resources, visit **www.Nutmoji.com**.

Book design by Sterling Chen

Main typography set in Bitter (Huerta Tipográfica); display type set in Amatic SC, (Vernon Adams, Ben Nathan, Thomas Jockin, Cyreal); captions set in Caveat (Impallari Type). All fonts available at fonts.google.com. On page 19, Peanut's handwriting used Sue Ellen Francisco (Kimberly Geswein), and Pistachio's used Ink Free (Steve Matteson). Illustrations and design done in SketchBook, InDesign, and Photoshop.